THE
DALAI
LAMA

HIS ESSENTIAL
WISDOM

EDITED BY
CAROL
KELLY-GANGI

FALL RIVER PRESS

New York

FALL RIVER PRESS

New York

An Imprint of Sterling Publishing Co., Inc.
1166 Avenue of the Americas
New York, NY 10036

ISBN 978-1-4351-6961-6

Distributed in Canada by Sterling Publishing Co., Inc.
c/o Canadian Manda Group, 664 Annette Street
Toronto, Ontario M6S 2C8, Canada
Distributed in the United Kingdom by GMC Distribution Services
Castle Place, 166 High Street, Lewes, East Sussex BN7 1XU, England
Distributed in Australia by NewSouth Books
University of New South Wales, Sydney, NSW 2052, Australia

For information about custom editions, special sales, and premium and corporate purchases,
please contact Sterling Special Sales at 800-805-5489 or specialsales@sterlingpublishing.com.

Manufactured in the United States of America

2 4 6 8 10 9 7 5 3 1

sterlingpublishing.com

Cover design by David Ter-Avanesyan

CONTENTS

Contents

To John Christopher and Emily Grace with love.

INTRODUCTION

Lhamo Thondup, the future 14th Dalai Lama, was born on July 6, 1935 in Taktser, Amdo, Tibet. He was the ninth child born to his mother but only the fifth child to survive. At that time, he had an elder sister, eighteen years older than him, and three elder brothers. The Dalai Lama's mother was said by him to be the kindest person he had ever known. She once gave the entire contents of her pantry to a famine-stricken family who arrived at her door from nearby China. The Dalai Lama recalls his father as a man with a quick temper though not one to hold grudges for very long. They lived on a small farm and used most of what they grew to feed their family. Though they were poor, the family was raised in an atmosphere of loving kindness.

In December of 1933, the 13th Dalai Lama, Thupten Gyatso, died in Lhasa at the age of fifty-seven. The government immediately formulated a search party to locate the new incarnation of the Dalai Lama. Through a series of signs, the search party was led to the monastery in Kumbum and ultimately to the house of Lhamo Thondup, who was nearly three years old. The leader of the search party, a lama disguised as a servant, observed the young child closely for the entire day. Despite the lama's disguise, the child was able to correctly identify him, calling out "Sera lama, Sera lama," Sera being the monastery to which the holy man belonged. The search party returned again bringing with them several items that had belonged to the 13th Dalai Lama along with items that did not. In each case, the child correctly chose the items that had belonged to the 13th Dalai Lama. After consideration of these and other signs, the search party became convinced that Lhamo Thondup was indeed the new incarnation of the Dalai Lama.

On February 22, 1940, Thondup was enthroned as the 14th Dalai Lama in Lhasa. Shortly thereafter, he was inducted as a novice monk and was renamed Jamphel Ngawang Lobsang Yeshe Tenzin Gyatso. He thus began his monastic education at the age of five. His curriculum was that which is customary for a monk studying for a doctorate in Buddhist philosophy. His formal education would continue for close to twenty years.

In October of 1950, an army of 80,000 from Communist China crossed over the border into Tibet. The situation worsened as the months wore on, and the people of Tibet began to advocate for the Dalai Lama to assume full temporal control of Tibet. After consideration by the highest levels of government and consultation with an oracle, it was agreed. On November 17, 1950, at the age of fifteen, the Dalai Lama assumed full temporal leadership of Tibet. He immediately appointed two new Prime Ministers and sent delegations abroad in the hopes of gaining international support for Tibet's position. However, in May of 1951, under sigificant duress, the so-called Seventeen-Point Agreement was reached between Tibet and China, which in effect, returned Tibet to the motherland of China.

In the years that followed, the Dalai Lama did all that he could to prevent a full takeover of Tibet by the Chinese, including an historic trip to China in July of 1954 where he met with Mao Zedong and other Chinese leaders for peace talks. By March of 1959, however, it became clear that the Dalai Lama's life was in danger. Thousands of Tibetans took to the streets and surrounded the palace in order to protect the life of their young leader. After consultation with his ministers and an oracle, the Dalai Lama came to the conclusion that he had to leave Tibet in order to prevent a fullscale massacre of the thousands of Tibetans who would fight to the death to save him. On March 17, 1959, the Dalai Lama, disguised as an ordinary soldier, slipped out of the gates of Norbulingka Palace with his Chamberlain, Abbot, and bodyguard, and began the three-week journey to the safety of India. Many thousands of Tibetan refugees followed him there.

Upon his arrival in India, the Dalai Lama immediately set out to meet with Indian officials and devised the plans necessary to rehabilitate the Tibetan refugees and provide for the education of their children and the preservation of the Tibetan religion and culture. He set up the government of Tibet in Exile and formally repudiated the Seventeen-Point Agreement.

Once under Chinese control, the Tibetan people were ruthlessly suppressed. Many thousands of Tibetans were executed, imprisoned, and sent to labor camps, and martial law was declared. During the Cultural Revolution that followed, the Chinese embarked on a plan to systematically destroy the religion of the Tibetan people. By 1976, only a small number of Tibet's more than 6,000 monasteries and convents were still standing. More than a quarter of a million monks and nuns were forced to leave the religious life and more than 100,000 were tortured and murdered.

For sixty years, the Dalai Lama in exile has worked tirelessly on behalf of Tibet and the six million Tibetans for which he is responsible. He made numerous appeals to the United Nations for the humane treatment of Tibetans by the Chinese. In 1987, the Dalai Lama proposed the

Five Point Peace Plan to Congress and expanded on the plan in 1988 in Strasbourg to members of the European Parliament. His "Middle Way" proposal offered the Chinese control of the foreign policy and defense of Tibet in exchange for internal autonomy. On December 10, 1989, the Dalai Lama was awarded the Nobel Peace Prize which he accepted "in a spirit of optimism" as he spoke of the reaffirmation of nonviolence, peace, and understanding between all members of the human race.

This book offers readers hundreds of inspiring quotations from the Dalai Lama. In these excerpts, His Holiness the Dalai Lama speaks with simple eloquence about the need for compassion and kindness; the search for happiness; the meaning of pain and suffering; the importance of family; the path to peace; the role of religion; and the challenges of life in the modern world. In other selections, the Dalai Lama recalls his singular childhood; the turmoil surrounding the Communist takeover of Tibet; and his years in exile.

At the age of eighty-three, the Dalai Lama continues to travel the globe wherever he is welcome to spread his undying message of kindness, love, and compassion to Buddhists and non-Buddhists alike. Though he is content to embrace the role of "a simple Buddhist monk," the Dalai Lama is universally recognized as a champion of world peace and human rights everywhere and one of the world's foremost spiritual leaders.

—Carol Kelly-Gangi
Rumson, New Jersey

EARLY YEARS

In the few months before I was born, my father himself had been badly ill and unable to get out of bed. Yet on the morning of my birth, he got up feeling perfectly well, and offered prayers and filled the butter lamps which always burned on our family altar. . . . When I was born, and my mother told him, "It's a boy," he simply said, "Good. I would like to make him a monk."

My mother gave birth to sixteen children, but nine of them died when they were very young. The whole family was linked together by the strongest bonds of love and kindness.

There they found the baby of the family, and the moment the little boy saw the lama, he went to him and wanted to sit on his lap. The lama was disguised in a cloak which was lined with lambskin, but round his neck he was wearing a rosary which had belonged to the Thirteenth Dalai Lama. The little boy seemed to recognize the rosary, and he asked to be given it. . . . The lama spent the whole day in watching the little boy with increasing interest, until it was time for the boy to be put to bed. All the party stayed in the house for the night, and early next morning, when they were making ready to leave, the boy got out of his bed and insisted that he wanted to go with them. I was that boy.

All this time, strict secrecy was observed on the whole matter, not only for fear of what the Chinese governor might do, but also because the discovery had not yet been laid before the National Assembly of Tibet for official acceptance. Not even my parents were told of the firm belief of the search party, and even through the long period of waiting, they never suspected that I might be the reincarnation of the highest of all lamas. However, my mother has told me since I grew up that there had been previous signs of some extraordinary fate for me.

This brought the ceremony to an end. It had been long, and I am told that everybody present had been delighted to see how, although young, I had been able to play my part with suitable dignity and composure. . . .Thus, when I was four-and-a-half-years old, I was formally recognized as the Fourteenth Dalai Lama, the spiritual and temporal ruler of Tibet. To all Tibetans, the future seemed happy and secure.

Like most children, I started by learning to read and write, and I felt what I suppose young boys of that age generally feel—a certain reluctance and some resistance. The idea of being tied down to books and the company of teachers was not very interesting. However, I found myself doing my lessons to my teachers' satisfaction, and as I got used to the strict course of study, they began to mark my progress as rather unusually rapid.

I worked hard at my religious education as a boy, but my life was not all work. I am told that some people in other countries believe the Dalai Lamas were almost prisoners in the Potala Palace. It is true that I could not go out very often because of my studies; but a house was built for my family between the Potala and the city of Lhasa, and I saw them at least every month or six weeks, so that I was not entirely cut off from family life.

Even as a child, I didn't care for formalities. I was especially close to the kitchen manager. From my servants, who treated me like any other little boy, I already learned quite early that life could be difficult for common folk. They told me that there were unjust government officials and lamas who often made very arbitrary decisions. At a young age, I recognized that the leader of a people needs to be connected with common folk.

One by one, other subjects were added to my curriculum, and as I went on I found less and less difficulty in learning all that was required of me. In fact, I began to feel a growing inquisitiveness to know more and more. My interest reached beyond my allotted studies, and I found satisfaction in reading advanced chapters of the books and wanting to know from my teachers more than I was supposed to at my age.

All in all, it was not an unhappy childhood. The kindness of my teachers will always remain with me as a memory I shall cherish. They gave me the religious knowledge which has always been and will always be my greatest comfort and inspiration, and they did their best to satisfy what they regarded as a healthy curiosity in other matters. But I know that I grew up with hardly any knowledge of worldly affairs, and it was in that state, when I was sixteen, that I was called upon to lead my country against the invasion of Communist China.

My dual position as Dalai Lama, by which Tibet had been happily ruled for centuries, was becoming almost insupportable. . . . Thus I began to think it might be in the best interests of Tibet if I withdrew from all political activities, in order to keep my religious authority intact. Yet while I was in Tibet, I could not escape from politics. To withdraw, I would have to leave the country, bitterly and desperately though I hated that idea. At that moment of the depth of my despondency, I received an invitation to visit India.

At dawn on 17 March 1959, the end was imminent. There were rumors of fresh troops arriving from China by air. For the exasperated crowd that surrounded the summer palace armed with sticks, knives, swords, and a few rifles, the Dalai Lama remained the most precious thing in the world. The crowd would stay there until the end, and would die in the hope of saving their "precious protector." It seemed that the situation was completely desperate. . . . I went out into the freezing night dressed in trousers and a long black cape, my glasses tucked away in my pocket. I slung a rifle on my shoulder, and was accompanied by two guards and my chamberlain. That is how I was able to walk through the gate unchallenged, like a humble soldier. And then my journey into exile began.

TEACHINGS OF BUDDHISM

A Buddhist is defined as one who seeks ultimate refuge in the Buddha, in his doctrine known as the Dharma, and in the Sangha, the spiritual community that practices according to that doctrine. These are known as the Three Jewels of Refuge.

The core teachings of the Buddha are grounded in the four noble truths. These are the foundation of the Buddhist teaching. The four noble truths are the truth of suffering, its origin, the possibility of cessation of suffering, and the path leading to that cessation. The teachings on the four noble truths are based in human experience, underlying which is the natural aspiration to seek happiness and to avoid suffering. The happiness that we desire and the suffering that we shun are not random but rather come about through causes and conditions.

Usually, when I describe the essence of Buddhism, I say that at best we should try to help others, and if we cannot help them at least we should do them no harm. This teaching grows from the soil of love and compassion.

It can rightly be asserted that loving-kindness and compassion are the two cornerstones on which the whole edifice of Buddhism stands. Destruction or injury to life is strictly forbidden. Harming or destroying any being from the highest to the lowest, from a human to the tiniest insect, must at all costs be avoided. The Blessed One said: "Do not harm others. Just as you feel affection on seeing a dearly beloved person, so should you extend loving-kindness to all creatures."

According to Buddhist practice, basically there are three stages or steps. The initial stage is to reduce attachment toward life. The second stage is the elimination of desire and attachment to this samsara. Then in the third stage, self-cherishing is eliminated. As a result of rigorous practice I feel there is a possibility of cessation; i.e., nirvana.

Buddhism is atheistic in the sense that a creator God is not accepted; rather, Buddhism presents a view of self-creation, that one's own actions create one's life situations. In this light, it has been said that Buddhism is not a religion, but a science of the mind.

We Buddhists live in a world without a god. For many of the others, the Creator God is the center of doctrine. But they all agree that love and compassion make people better. For our religion, *mahakaruna*, the great healing kindness toward all sentient beings, is the most important thing.

Buddhism states that man is his own master, or that he has the potential to become his own master. This is the very basis of Buddhist philosophy and we have developed considerable experience of a great number of different methods in order to reach self-mastery. Mind is the creator of our world, in every moment. That is why responsibility is so crucially connected with our mind.

For us, the focus is not on God but on enlightenment. Human beings are responsible for their own lives. We alone are the creators of our fate. The Buddha did not create the world, nor is he responsible for its deficiencies. But he shows us ways in which we can move from the present state of suffering to perfection. Because of this and other reasons, the Buddha did not address teachings about the existence of God.

In Buddhism we have the concept of *bodhichitta*, the spirit of enlightenment. This denotes an aspiration to realize Buddhahood in order to bring about good for all beings, and it is equivalent to the notion of universal responsibility. From my own personal experience, it is a great help to think about the spirit of enlightenment when we are sad or our mind is disturbed. If we think about taking on a great responsibility when we are troubled or confused, our mind opens, relaxes, and becomes stronger.

The practice of morality, which means guarding your three doors of body, speech, and mind from indulging in unwholesome activities, equips you with mindfulness and conscientiousness. Therefore, morality is the foundation of the Buddhist path.

The highest form of spiritual practice is the cultivation of the altruistic intention to attain enlightenment for the benefit of all sentient beings, known as *bodhichitta*. This is the most precious state of mind, the supreme source of benefit and goodness, that which fulfills both our immediate and ultimate aspirations, and the basis of altruistic activity. However, bodhichitta can only be realized through regular concerted effort, so in order to attain it we need to cultivate the discipline necessary for training and transforming our mind.

The Buddha attained total purification of his mind, speech, and body. We consider that before his enlightenment he was a man like any other. It was through his own efforts that he became the Buddha. And after reaching complete enlightenment, he gave an enormous number of teachings responding to our many interests and concerns, with the aim of liberating all living beings from suffering. . . . He also taught that our future is in our own hands, not in the hands of God nor in the hands of the Buddha.

The principal physical nonvirtues are killing, stealing, and sexual misconduct; the principal verbal nonvirtues are lying, divisive talk, harsh speech, and senseless chatter; the principal mental nonvirtues are covetousness, harmful intent, and wrong views. These ten cause suffering both for others and for you.

Buddhism is one of the many religions which teaches us to be less selfish and more compassionate. It teaches us to be humane, altruistic, and to think of others in the way we think of ourselves. Our daily thoughts and actions should be directed toward the benefit of others.

In the Buddha Dharma, particularly in the Mahayana tradition or the Sanskrit tradition, all sentient beings have a Buddha nature. So when we face problems dealing with other people, we remember that they are sentient beings just like us and have a Buddha nature. The ultimate nature of everyone is pure. This belief will calm our mind and will reduce negative feelings.

Converting other people to Buddhism is not my concern. I am interested in how we Buddhists can contribute to human society. The Buddha gave us an example of contentment and tolerance, through serving others unselfishly. I believe that his teaching and example can still contribute to global peace and individual happiness.

For certain people, Buddhism may simply not be an answer. Different religions meet different people's needs. I do not try to convert people to Buddhism. What I try to explore is how we Buddhists can make a contribution to human society in accordance with our ideas and values.

What is our goal? Actually, Buddhists should save all beings. Even if we can't expand our thinking so as to include beings living in other worlds, we ought to take all human beings on this planet into consideration, and in this way we have a practical starting point.

COMPASSION

Love based on attachment is limited and precarious. It mainly involves projection. Imagine, for example, that a very attractive person appears and you are immediately drawn to them. Today you are in love, but tomorrow it is quite possible that your feelings will turn hostile. Love based on attachment is of no real help. What does it bring us, if not irritation and annoyance? We believe that true compassion is free of attachment. This compassion is expressed spontaneously and unconditionally, like that of a mother who expects nothing from her child in return. It is such a demanding form of love that it gives birth to an indomitable desire to make all beings happy.

Compassion can be roughly defined in terms of a state of mind that is nonviolent and nonharming, or nonaggressive. Because of this there is a danger of confusing compassion with attachment and intimacy.

Compassion is compulsory for everyone to practice, and if I were a dictator I would dictate to everyone to do so.

It must be said that genuine compassion is not like pity or a feeling that others are somehow lower than you. Rather, with genuine compassion you view others as more important than yourself.

I have found that the greatest degree of inner tranquility comes from the development of love and compassion. The more we care for the happiness of others, the greater is our own sense of well-being. Cultivating a close, warmhearted feeling for others automatically puts the mind at ease. It is the ultimate source of success in life.

There are a number of qualities which are important for mental peace, but from the little experience I have, I believe that one of the most important factors is human compassion and affection: a sense of caring.

In the case of one individual or person like myself, the practice of compassion and religion coincides. But another individual, without religion, can practice spirituality without being religious. So, a secular person can be spiritual.

Genuine compassion should be unbiased. If we only feel close to our friends, and not to our enemies, or to the countless people who are unknown to us personally and toward whom we are indifferent, then our compassion is only partial or biased.

Sometimes when people hear about the Buddhist practice of detachment, they think that Buddhism is advocating indifference toward all things, but that is not the case. Cultivating detachment takes the sting out of our emotions toward others that are based on superficial considerations of distance or closeness. Then, on that basis, we can develop a compassion that is truly universal.

True compassion is not just an emotional response but a firm commitment founded on reason. Therefore, a truly compassionate attitude toward others does not change even if they behave negatively. Through universal altruism, you develop a feeling of responsibility for others: the wish to help them actively overcome their problems.

Compassion

As a result of your continuous meditation and contemplation, your feeling of compassion toward other sentient beings will become as intense as the love of a mother toward her only child when she sees him or her suffering from an illness. The child's suffering would cause her worry and pain, and day and night she would have the natural wish that her son or daughter be well.

According to Buddhism the life of all beings—human, animal, or otherwise—is precious, and all have the same right to happiness. For this reason I find it disgraceful that animals are used without being shown the slightest compassion, and that they are used for scientific experiments. . . . I have also noticed that those who lack any compassion for animals and who do not hesitate to kill them are also those who, sooner or later, show a lack of compassion toward human beings.

Generating concern for others has vast power to transform your mind. If you practice compassion for the sake of all living beings—including animals—then that same limitless merit will accrue to you.

LOVE

Love is the center of human life.

Without love we could not survive. Human beings are social creatures, and a concern for each other is the very basis of our life together.

The Buddhist definition of love is the wish that all sentient beings may enjoy happiness and never be parted from happiness.

If you have love and compassion toward all sentient beings, particularly toward your enemy, that is true love and compassion. Now, the kind of love or compassion that you have toward your friends, your wife, and your children is essentially not true kindness. That is attachment. That kind of love cannot be infinite.

The feeling of a mother for her child is a classic example of love. For the safety, protection, and welfare of her children, a mother is ready to sacrifice her very life. Recognizing this, children should be grateful to their mothers and express their gratitude by performing virtuous deeds.

During the initial period of human life, love is also one of the most important preconditions for the balanced development of human nature. If it is missing, then people feel insecure throughout their lives and are plagued by all kinds of fears.

If there is love, there is hope to have real families, real brotherhood, real equanimity, real peace. If the love within your mind is lost, if you continue to see other beings as enemies, then no matter how much knowledge or education you have, no matter how much material progress is made, only suffering and confusion will ensue.

The actual sequence of meditation on love is that first you should cultivate love directed toward your own friends and relatives, then you should shift that attention to neutral persons, then on to your enemies as well. Then gradually include all other sentient beings whom you encounter.

From the Buddhist perspective loving-kindness says that we truly take the other person seriously. The love must also be uninhibited and must not stop with the sympathy that we feel for our friends or our own family. It must include our enemies.

Once you recognize all other beings as your kind, dear mothers then naturally you will feel close to them. With this as a basis, you should cultivate love or loving-kindness, which is traditionally defined as the wish to see others enjoy happiness, and then you also develop compassion, which is the wish for others to be free of suffering. Love and compassion are two sides of the same coin.

The process of expanding love begins with developing equanimity, after which the main point is not whether a particular person is good or bad to you but the fact that the person is the same as yourself in wanting happiness and not wanting suffering. Since this desire resides in all sentient beings, your awareness of it can apply to everyone, making the basis of your love very stable. Once you put the emphasis on their similarity to yourself, love has a solid foundation that does not vacillate depending on temporary circumstances.

Right from the moment of our birth, we are under the care and kindness of our parents and then later on in our life when we are oppressed by sickness and become old, we are again dependent on the kindness of others. Since at the beginning and end of our lives we are so dependent on others' kindness, how can it be that in the middle we neglect kindness toward others?

It is necessary to help others, not only in our prayers, but in our daily lives. If we find we cannot help others, the least we can do is to desist from harming them.

Having a heart, and a kind and warm disposition, is an enormous advantage. Not only does it bring us joy, but we can share this joy with others. Relations between individuals, nations, and continents deteriorate only from lack of goodwill and kindness, even though these qualities are so valuable and necessary for the quality of life in society. That is why it is worth trying to develop them.

Love

Love is a simple practice yet it is very beneficial for the individual who practices it as well as for the community in which he lives, for the nation, and for the whole world.

In daily practice, reflect on the benefits of love, compassion, kindness, and so forth, then reflect on the disadvantages of anger. Such continuous thoughtful contemplation, the growing appreciation of love, revivifying and increasing—all have the effect of lessening our affinity for hatred and gaining our respect for love.

KINDNESS AND FRIENDSHIP

I am quite sure that if this Fourteenth Dalai Lama smiled less, perhaps I would have fewer friends in various places. My attitude towards other people is to always look at them from the human level. On that level, whether president, queen or beggar, there is no difference, provided that there is genuine human feeling with a genuine human smile of affection.

If someone greets me with a nice smile, and expresses a genuinely friendly attitude, I appreciate it very much. Though I might not know that person or understand their language, they instantly gladden my heart. . . . Kindness and love, a real sense of brotherhood and sisterhood, these are very precious. They make community possible and thus are crucial in society.

Loving oneself is crucial. If we do not love ourselves, how can we love others? It seems that when some people talk of compassion, they have the notion that it entails a total disregard for one's own interests—a sacrificing of one's interests. This is not the case. In fact genuine love should first be directed at oneself.

The foundation of all spiritual practice is love. That you practice this well is my only request. Of course, to be able to do so in all situations will take time, but you should not lose courage. If we wish happiness for mankind, love is the only way.

So to those who say that the Dalai Lama is being unrealistic in advocating this ideal of unconditional love, I urge them to experiment with it nonetheless. They will discover that when we reach beyond the confines of narrow self-interest, our hearts become filled with strength. Peace and joy become our constant companion.

Our life is not very long: one hundred years or so at the most. If throughout its duration, we try to be kind, warmhearted, and concerned about the welfare of others, and less selfish and angry, that will be wonderful, excellent; that is really the cause of happiness. If you are selfish and always put yourself first and others second, you will finish last. If mentally, you put yourself last and others first, you will come out ahead.

The moment we think of ourselves—me—we are very self-centered and narrow-minded. Our area of operation becomes very small. Under such circumstances, even small problems appear to loom large, be unbearable, and generate more worry and anxiety. On the other hand, the moment one thinks about the welfare of other beings, one's mind automatically widens.

I think human beings are the superior sentient beings on this planet. Humans have the potential not only to create happy lives for themselves, but also to help other beings. We have a natural creative ability and it is very important to realize this.

The practice of cultivating altruism has a beneficial effect not only from the religious point of view but also from the mundane point of view, not only for long-term spiritual development but even in terms of immediate rewards. From my own personal experience I can tell you that when I practice altruism and care for others, it immediately makes me calmer and more secure. So altruism brings immediate benefits.

We are, after all, social animals. Without human friendship, without the human smile, our lives become miserable. The loneliness becomes unbearable. Such human interdependence is a natural law—that is to say, according to natural law, we depend on others to live.

Genuine human friendship is on the basis of human affection, irrespective of your position. Therefore, the more you show concern about the welfare and rights of others, the more you are a genuine friend. The more you remain open and sincere, then ultimately more benefits will come to you. If you forget or do not bother about others, then eventually you will lose your own benefits.

Developing a warm heart ourselves can also transform others. As we become nicer human beings, our neighbors, friends, parents, spouses, and children experience less anger. They will become more warm-hearted, compassionate, and harmonious. The very atmosphere becomes happier, which promotes good health, perhaps even a longer life.

Friends, genuine friends, have much to do with a warm heart, not money, not power. When you gain wealth, political power, or fame, you may find friends of a different sort—but these are not necessarily genuine friends. A genuine friend considers you just as another human being, as a brother or sister, and shows affection on that level, regardless of whether you are rich or poor, in a high position or a low position. That is a genuine friend.

If you want a genuine friend, we must create a positive atmosphere. After all, we are social animals. I think in our life friends are very important, as are a friendly manner and genuine smile.

Since beginningless time, in the course of rebirths which must be infinite in number, every being has been included within your sphere of existence, and has established a relationship with you just like the one you enjoy with your mother in this life. You must make this your strong conviction. And on the basis of this understanding, you will gradually begin to consider all beings as friends.

Of course, it is natural and right that we all want friends. But is friendship produced through quarrels and anger, jealousy and intense competitiveness? I do not think so. The best way to make friends is to be very compassionate! Only affection brings us genuine close friends. You should take care of others, be concerned for their welfare, help them, serve them, make more friends, make more smiles. The result? When you yourself need help, you'll find plenty of helpers! If, on the other hand, you neglect the happiness of others, in the long term you will be the loser.

Now let us look at the last moment of our lives—death. Even at the time of death, although the dying person can no longer benefit much from his friends, if he is surrounded by friends his mind may be more calm. Therefore throughout our lives, from the very beginning right up to our death, human affection plays a very important role.

HAPPINESS

Love, compassion, and concern for others are real sources of
happiness. With these in abundance, you will not be disturbed
by even the most uncomfortable circumstances. If you nurse
hatred, however, you will not be happy even in the lap of luxury.
Thus, if we really want happiness, we must widen the sphere of
love. This is both religious thinking and basic common sense.

What brings about happiness? Happiness is related to the way we
think. If we do not train our minds, and do not reflect on life, it is
impossible to find happiness.

Unless our minds are stable and calm, no matter how comfortable
our physical condition may be, they will give us no pleasure.
Therefore, the key to a happy life, now and in the future, is to
develop a happy mind.

Human happiness and human satisfaction must ultimately come from within oneself. It is wrong to expect some final satisfaction to come from money or from a computer.

Happiness is a state of mind. With physical comforts if your mind is still in a state of confusion and agitation, it is not happiness. Happiness means calmness of mind.

The sense of contentment is a key factor for attaining happiness. Bodily health, material wealth and companions and friends are three factors for happiness. Contentment is the key that will determine the outcome of your relations with all three of these factors.

All living beings, starting from insects, want happiness and not suffering. However, we are only one, whereas others are infinite in number. Thus, it can be clearly decided that others gaining happiness is more important than just yourself alone.

Foolish selfish people are always thinking of themselves, and the result is always negative. Wise persons think of others, helping them as much as they can, and the result is happiness.

We are all part of humanity, and each of us has the responsibility to improve humanity and to bring it additional happiness in order to make it more peaceful, friendlier, and compassionate. So, if one individual practices compassion and forgiveness sincerely and regularly, wherever he or she may live, it will generate a positive atmosphere. That is a way to contribute toward the betterment of humanity.

In this world, all qualities spring from preferring the wellbeing of others to our own, whereas frustrations, confusion, and pain result from selfish attitudes. By adopting an altruistic outlook and by treating others in the way they deserve, our own happiness is assured as a byproduct. We should realize that self-centeredness is the source of all suffering, and that thinking of others is the source of all happiness.

Generally speaking, Tibetans are also known for being joyful. "What is your secret?" is the question I am asked time and again about this. Whether we are educated or illiterate, we are used to thinking of all living beings as "our mothers and fathers." These are the terms that were always used in Tibet. I feel that it is our identification with the compassionate ideal that is at the source of our good-naturedness and our sense of joy.

I am always quite cheerful! I think, the result of my own practice and training. In my lifetime, I have lost my country and have been reduced to being totally dependent on the goodwill of others. . . . Of course these are tragic incidents, and I feel sad when I think about them. However, I don't feel overwhelmed by sadness. Old, familiar faces disappear, and new faces appear, but I still maintain my happiness and peace of mind.

KARMA

Pleasure and pain come from your own past actions. So it is easy to define *karma* in one short sentence. "Act well, and things will go well; act wrongly, and things will go wrong."

If more people believed in the law of karma, we would never need a police force or peace treaties. But without an inner conviction that nobody can escape the consequences of their actions, even if we employ many types of external means in order to enforce the law, we will never be able to build a peaceful society. . . . If human society is to improve, it is not enough to enforce external laws. We need to have recourse to our inner judge.

Bad karma can be weakened through repentance. The bad deed must be repented of, with the firm intention of not doing it again. We can be liberated from the incessant cycle of birth, suffering, death, and rebirth only when our entire negative karma has been extinguished. In other words, only when we have freed ourselves from all worldly desires can we achieve Buddhahood.

The notion of karma especially shows us that we are responsible for our own fate and should take charge of our own lives. We believe that the intention is what primarily counts. As long as we want to do good, even if the result is bad there will be no unfavorable effects. On the other hand, when we do nothing even when someone is dependent on our help, this can lead to karmic entanglements.

Everything that individual beings experience depends on their good or bad motives. They are the root of our actions and our experiences. Karma also has a metaphysical and an ethical aspect. Bad karma must be rendered ineffective through good deeds, through a good life.

One of the characteristics of karmic theory is that there is a definite, commensurate relationship between cause and effect. There is no way that negative actions or unwholesome deeds can result in joy and happiness. Joy and happiness, by definition, are the results or fruits of wholesome actions. So from that point of view, it is possible for us to admire not so much the immediate action, but the real causes of joy.

According to Buddhist scriptures, the creator of the world as we know now is nothing other than the ripening force of our own previous deeds or karma. Every action we ever create establishes an imprint on the mind that can contribute to our future evolution.

What do people understand a good life to be? It cannot be equated with a pleasant life in which all of our material wishes and dreams are fulfilled. Instead, it is a life lived in ethical responsibility. A life in which we do not think only of our own well-being but also serve others. Good karma is created only through good deeds. As a result of doing good, we become better persons and find a truly superior place in this life and the next life. We reach a higher level on the path to nirvana.

Make efforts to consider as transitory all adverse circumstances and disturbances. Like ripples in a pool, they occur and soon disappear. Insofar as our lives are karmically conditioned, they are characterized by endless cycles of problems. One problem appears and passes, and soon another one begins.

ANGER AND FORGIVENESS

If the basic human nature was aggressive, we would have been born with animal claws and huge teeth—but ours are very short, very pretty, very weak! That means we are not well equipped to be aggressive beings. Even the size of our mouth is very small. So I think the basic nature of human beings should be gentle.

I do not agree with people who assert that human beings are innately aggressive, despite the apparent prevalence of anger and hatred in the world. It is obvious that there never will be a perfect humanity. What we can achieve is that increasingly more people are willing to be part of the conversation, and that they behave in a more tolerant and peaceful manner. This will push back destructive forces. This alone would be progress.

Anger and hatred are our real enemies. They are the forces we most need to confront and defeat, not the temporary "enemies" who appear intermittently throughout our life. And unless we train our minds to reduce their negative force, they will continue to disturb us and disrupt our attempts to develop a calm mind.

Under the power of anger or attachment we commit all kinds of harmful acts—often having far-reaching and destructive consequences. A person gripped by such states of mind and emotion is like a blind person, who cannot see where he is going. Yet we neglect to challenge these negative thoughts and emotions that lead us nearly to insanity. On the contrary, we often nurture and reinforce them! By doing this we are, in fact, making ourselves prey to their destructive power. When you reflect along these lines, you will realize that our true enemy is not outside ourselves.

When negative thoughts and motivations such as hatred or anger are present, even a friend is seen as an enemy, but when negative thoughts toward an enemy disappear, the enemy becomes a friend.

When I was young, I became angry easily. This may run in my family, because my father had a similar temperament. But today it is possible for me to control my fits of anger through spiritual mental exercises. We should not stop exercising our mind, because that is the only way for the intellect to differentiate between what is beneficial for it and what harms it. In order to strengthen this attitude within myself, I visualize the following image time and again: I am standing alone, and facing me is a large crowd of people. And I ask myself: Whose interests are more important? My own, or those of the countless other people?

Giving your anger the instrument of words and actions is like giving a child a pile of straw and a box of matches. Once lit, anger feeds off the air of exposure and can rage out of control. The only alternative is to control anger, and the way to do this is to think, What is the value of anger? What is the value of tolerance and compassion?

We all have a nature of suffering and impermanence. Once we recognize our community in deprivation, there is no sense in being belligerent with each other. Consider a group of prisoners who are about to be executed. During their stay together in prison, all of them will meet their end. There is no sense in quarreling out their remaining days. All of us are bound by the same nature of suffering and impermanence. Under such circumstances, there is absolutely no reason to fight with each other.

Your mental state should always remain calm. Even if some anxiety occurs, as it is bound to in life, you should always be calm. Like a wave, which rises from the water and dissolves back into the water, these disturbances are very short, so they should not affect your basic mental attitude. If you remain calm your blood pressure and so on remains more normal and as a result your health will improve.

You do not have to intentionally stop the various thoughts and feelings that dawn in the mind; rather, do not get caught up in them, do not let your mind be drawn into them. The mind will then take on its own natural form, and its clear light nature can be identified. Then its basic purity can be known.

At times in our lives, our minds hold on to anger and attachment, and at other times to detachment, contentment, love, and compassion. We cannot feel desire and hatred at exactly the same time toward the very same object. We can certainly have these feelings at different times, but not in the very same moment, which shows that these two attitudes function in contradiction to each other. When one of them increases in strength, the other decreases.

It would be much more constructive if people tried to understand their supposed enemies. Learning to forgive is much more useful than merely picking up a stone and throwing it at the object of one's anger, the more so when the provocation is extreme. For it is under the greatest adversity that there exists the greatest potential for doing good, both for oneself and others.

When we are able to recognize and forgive ignorant actions done in one's past, we strengthen ourselves and can solve the problems of the present constructively.

Anger cannot be overcome by anger. If a person shows anger to you, and you show anger in return, the result is a disaster. In contrast, if you control your anger and show its opposite—love, compassion, tolerance, and patience—then not only will you remain in peace, but the anger of others also will gradually diminish.

When I compare my temperament now to the way it was when I was between the ages of fifteen and twenty, I see a noticeable difference. These days, I hardly find myself being irritated at all, and even when I am, it doesn't last long. This is a marvelous benefit of my own practice and training—now I am always quite cheerful!

PAIN, SUFFERING, AND PATIENCE

If you have fear of some pain or suffering, you should examine whether there is anything you can do about it. If you can, there is no need to worry about it; if you cannot do anything, then also there is no need to worry.

If you see that some situation or person is going to cause you suffering, it is important to engage in techniques to avoid it; but once suffering has started, it should be received not as a burden but as something that can assist you. Undergoing small sufferings in this lifetime can purify the karma of many ill deeds accumulated in former lifetimes. Adopting this perspective will help you see the ills of cyclic existence, and the more you can do this, the more you will dislike engaging in nonvirtues.

Suffering originates from various causes and conditions. But the root cause of our pain and suffering lies in our own ignorant and undisciplined state of mind. The happiness we seek can be attained only through the purification of our minds.

The observation that good people suffer, and evil people keep enjoying benefits and recognition, is shortsighted. Also, this kind of conclusion might have been made in haste. If one analyzes carefully, one finds that troublemakers are definitely not happy. It is better to behave well and take responsibility for one's actions, and lead a positive life.

Encountering sufferings will definitely contribute to the elevation of your spiritual practice, provided you are able to transform the calamity and misfortune into the path.

Suffering can also be a school of life. When we look at the biographies of influential people, we see that in many cases they become much stronger precisely because of difficult experiences. Someone who is pampered and has everything can fall into deep despair when even the smallest difficulties arise.

In my case, at the age of sixteen I lost my freedom, and at twenty-four I lost my country. I have been a refugee for the past forty years, with heavy responsibilities. As I look back, my life has not been easy. However, throughout all these years, I learned about compassion, about caring for others. This mental attitude has brought me inner strength.

Through a difficult period you can learn to develop inner strength, determination, and courage to face the problem. If you become discouraged, that is the real failure; you have lost a valuable chance to develop. . . . When things go smoothly, life can easily become like an official ceremony in which protocol, like how you walk and how you speak, is more important than content. But at a time of crisis these things are pointless—you have to deal with reality and become more practical.

Hard times build determination and inner strength. Through them we can also come to appreciate the uselessness of anger. Instead of getting angry, nurture a deep caring and respect for troublemakers because by creating such trying circumstances, they provide us with invaluable opportunities to practice tolerance and patience.

It is also worth remembering that the time of greatest gain in terms of wisdom and inner strength is often that of greatest difficulty. With the right approach—and here we see once more the supreme importance of developing a positive attitude—the experience of suffering can open our eyes to reality. For example, my own experience of life as a refugee has helped me realize that the endless protocol, which was such an important part of my life in Tibet, was quite unnecessary.

There is an Indian saying: "When an arrow has hit, there is no time to ask who shot it, or what kind of arrow it was." Similarly, when we encounter human suffering, it is important to respond with commiseration rather than to question the politics of those we help. Instead of asking whether their country is enemy or friend, we must think, these are human beings; they are suffering, and they have a right to happiness equal to our own.

In dealing with those who are undergoing great suffering, if you feel "burnout" setting in, if you feel demoralized and exhausted, it is best, for the sake of everyone, to withdraw and restore yourself. The point is to have a long-term perspective.

If we are very forbearing, then something we would normally consider very painful will not appear so bad after all. But without patient endurance, even the smallest thing becomes unbearable. A lot depends on our attitude.

There are different types of patience: the patience of being indifferent to the harm inflicted by others, the patience of voluntarily accepting hardship, and the patience developed through reasoned conviction in the Dharma.

Tolerance and patience with courage are not signs of failure but signs of victory. In your daily life, as you learn more patience, more tolerance with wisdom and courage, you will see it is the true source of success.

Patience is the countermeasure for mental dissatisfaction. Greed and its self-centeredness—I want this, I want that—brings unhappiness and also destruction of the environment, exploitation of others, and increases the gap between the rich and the poor. The countermeasure is contentment.

Pain, Suffering, and Patience

The most important benefit of *sö pa*, or patience, consists in the way it acts as a powerful antidote to the affliction of anger—the greatest threat to our inner peace, and therefore our happiness. Indeed, we find that patience is the best means we have of defending ourselves internally from anger's destructive effects.

Without enemies you could not fully engage in the practice of patience—tolerance and forbearance. We need enemies, and should be grateful to them. From the viewpoint of training in altruism, an enemy is really your guru, your teacher; only an enemy can teach you tolerance. An enemy is the greatest teacher of altruism, and for that reason, instead of hating, we must respect him.

We are human beings—one of our better qualities is our ability to think and judge. If we lose patience and get angry, we lose our ability to make proper judgments and thereby lose one of the most powerful instruments we have for tackling problems: our wisdom.

MEDITATION

In my own meditation practice I am mainly concerned with
compassion, with the differentiation between the self and others
and with the way all things and living beings, especially human
beings, are interdependent on each other. I pray, meditate, or study
every day for at least five and a half hours. I also pray during the
rest of the day whenever I get the chance. We have prayers for
everything that we do. For Buddhists, there is hardly any
distinction between religion and everyday life.

What do we understand by meditation? From the Buddhist
point of view, meditation is a spiritual discipline, and one that
allows you to have some degree of control over your thoughts and
emotions. Why is it that we don't succeed in enjoying the lasting
happiness that we are seeking? Buddhism explains that our normal
state of mind is such that our thoughts and emotions are wild
and unruly, and since we lack the mental discipline needed to
tame them, we are powerless to control them. As a result, they
control us. And thoughts and emotions, in their turn, tend to be
controlled by our negative impulses rather than our positive ones.
We need to reverse this cycle.

Meditation

Meditation is the process whereby we gain control over the mind and guide it in a more virtuous direction. Meditation may be thought of as a technique by which we diminish the force of old thought habits and develop new ones. We thereby protect ourselves from engaging in actions of mind, word or deed that lead to our suffering. Such meditation is to be used extensively in our spiritual practice.

When we use meditation on our spiritual path, it is to familiarize ourselves with a chosen object. This object need not be a physical thing such as an image of the Buddha or Jesus on the cross. The "chosen object" can be a mental quality such as patience, which we work at cultivating within ourselves by means of meditative contemplation. It can also be the rhythmic movement of our breath, which we focus on to still our restless minds. And it can be the mere quality of clarity and knowing—our consciousness—the nature of which we seek to understand.

At a time when people are so conscious of maintaining their physical health by controlling their diets, exercising, and so forth, it makes sense to try to cultivate the corresponding positive mental attitudes too.

For a meditator who has a certain degree of inner stability and realization, every experience comes as a teaching; every event, every experience one is exposed to comes as a kind of learning experience.

Whatever forms of meditation you practice, the most important point is to apply mindfulness continuously, and make a sustained effort. It is unrealistic to expect results from meditation within a short period of time. What is required is continuous sustained effort.

As a technique to identify the basic nature of the mind, first stop remembering what happened in the past, then stop thinking about what might happen in the future; let the mind flow of its own accord without the overlay of thought. Let the mind rest in its natural state and observe it for a while.

It is easier to meditate than to actually do something for others. Sometimes I feel that to merely meditate on compassion is to take the passive option. Our meditation should form the basis for action, for seizing the opportunity to do something. The mediator's motivation, his sense of universal responsibility, should be expressed in deeds.

To develop genuine devotion, you must know the meaning of teachings. The main emphasis in Buddhism is to transform the mind, and transformation depends on meditation. In order to meditate correctly you must have knowledge, and communities, too, must be uplifted through knowledge.

SPEAKING TO FAMILY AND YOUTH

On the subject of love and marriage, my simple opinion is that making love is alright, but for marriage, don't hurry, be cautious. Make sure you will remain together forever, or at least for this whole life. If you do, then your union can be a happy one. A happy home is one step towards a happy world.

Kindness is the key to peace and harmony in family life. Families in exile must educate their children. They should be their first lama.

Loving-kindness toward a newborn child is the precondition for the child to develop properly on the spiritual and physical levels. This even applies to the period before an infant can understand the meaning of words.

Nearly all of us receive our first lessons in peaceful living from our mothers, because the need for love lies at the very foundation of human existence. From the earliest stages of our growth, we are completely dependent on our mother's care and it is very important for us that she express her love. If children do not receive proper affection, in later life they will often find it hard to love others.

Parents must provide not only outer warmth for their child but also inner warmth. They must create an atmosphere with a sense of security in which the child feels love and acceptance.

I have been very moved to find that the way we look after children in their earliest years has a big impact on the rest of their lives. On the one hand, a child needs adequate food, but on the other hand, without the tender care and affection of its parents, it will not reach full maturation. This has been shown through scientific research.

We are all born helpless. Without a parent's kindness we could not survive, much less prosper. When children grow up in constant fear, with no one to rely on, they suffer their whole lives. Because the minds of small children are very delicate, their need for kindness is particularly obvious.

Where children lack human affection and love, physical development is sometimes difficult as is study. So then I think the most important thing is that those children who had difficulties at an early age growing under the lack of human love and affection will find it difficult to show other humans love and compassion. And that's a great tragedy, a great tragedy.

Wise parents, without any anger, may sometimes scold or even punish their children. This is permissible, but if you really get angry and whack the child too much, then you will feel regret in the future. However, with a good motivation of seeking a child's welfare, it is possible to display an expression appropriate to what the child needs at that moment.

Once two parents are warmhearted and peaceful and calm persons, then their children eventually develop that kind of behavior. So, therefore I think the individual, the happy individual human beings, is very important.

The home environment is also important because children learn negative behavior from their parents. If, for example, the father is always getting into fights with his associates, or if the father and mother are always arguing destructively, although at first the child may find this objectionable, eventually they will come to understand it as quite normal. This learning is then taken out of the home and into the world.

Children are naturally warm-hearted and kind, but certain aspects of the education they receive increase the divisions among them, and this has the effect of creating a gap between one child and others. It seems very important, therefore, that along with education this basic kindness, found in its natural state in children, must be fostered. By this I mean that education should be in harmony with the child's essentially kind nature. The most important element is that children be raised in a climate of love and tenderness.

I believe that family planning is important. Of course, I do not mean to suggest we should not have children. Human life is a precious resource, and married couples should have children unless there are compelling reasons not to. The idea of not having children just because we want to enjoy a full life without responsibility is, I think, quite mistaken. At the same time, couples do have a duty to consider the impact our numbers have on the natural environment.

A limit to the size of the family is desirable. We have to take care of birth control. It is very, very essential to have fewer children, and those children must be properly taken care of. Besides education, one must introduce to them the reverence for life and the value of human affection.

There are two kinds of caring. If you just think of your family exclusively and do not bother about other sentient beings, that is attachment. But if you practice caring for all sentient beings, your family too becomes a part of these sentient beings. Also, you can communicate directly on this basis when you are taking care of your family members.

Among the 5.7 billion human beings, the older generation, including me, is getting ready to say goodbye to this world. The youth has to carry the responsibility for the future. So, please realize your responsibility, remember your potential, and have self-confidence. Have an open mind and a sense of caring and belonging. The freshness and strength that youth has should not fade away. You must keep this enthusiasm.

I place all of my hopes in the younger generation. The responsibility for the future lies with the youth. Young people today are exposed to many bad influences through the mass media. If young people see too much violence on television, this will certainly affect their behavior. Such unpleasant pictures can cause great harm to young people. We must seriously ask ourselves what must be done so that our young people receive a balanced education.

Plainly speaking, when I began speaking about the value of human beings, universal human values, and compassionate society, I did not really expect a response from the younger generation, and certainly not with such a deep commitment. I very much appreciate that young people have decided to help me to work for basic human rights for all humanity, and respect for human dignity. Of course, this movement is not easy, and there may be many obstacles, not necessarily due to direct opposition, but due to indifference, people being indifferent to basic human values.

I really have hoped and prayed that the younger generation in this world would take up the cause of truth and nonviolence. I believe that young people have a natural enthusiasm for truth, honesty, and peace. It is basic human nature for young people, who have minds that are very fresh, to have such an inclination.

LIFE, DEATH,
AND REBIRTH

We are all on this planet together. We are all brothers and sisters with the same physical and mental faculties, the same problems, and the same needs. We must all contribute to the fulfillment of the human potential and the improvement of the quality of life as much as we are able. Mankind is crying out for help. Ours is a desperate time. Those who have something to offer should come forward. Now is the time.

One great question underlies our experience, whether we think about it consciously or not: what is the purpose of life? From the moment of birth, every human being wants happiness and does not want suffering. Neither social conditioning nor education nor ideology affects this. From the very core of our being, we simply desire contentment. Therefore, it is important to discover what will bring about the greatest degree of happiness.

Whether as a monk or as the head of state, for me the meaning of life is to help others—especially the six million Tibetans who place all their hopes in me. As a result, I carry considerable responsibility on my shoulders. Of course, I primarily see my mission as helping my people and serving them with my total dedication. When we sincerely help others, we benefit doubly because at the same time we make ourselves happy.

The purpose of our life is to feel happiness, joy, satisfaction, and peace. In order to achieve that, so much depends on our mental attitude rather than money, power, or external things.

Try to develop a deep conviction that the present human body has great potential and that you shall never waste even a single moment of its use. . . . It is very wrong for people to feel deeply sad when they lose some money, yet when they waste the precious moments of their lives they do not have the slightest feeling of repentance.

The crux of our existence is that, as human beings, we live purposeful, meaningful lives. Our purpose is to develop a warm heart. We find meaning in being a friend to everyone. The sole source of peace in the family, the country, and the world is altruism—love and compassion.

If you are mindful of death, it will not come as a surprise—you will not be anxious. You will feel that death is merely like changing your clothes. Consequently, at that point you will be able to maintain your calmness of mind.

It is useless to be attached to this life, because even if we live for one hundred years we will have to die one day. Furthermore, we do not know the hour of our death: it could happen any time. And then our life will have to unravel, and however loved or wealthy we are, we will have no choice. What use will our belongings be to us then?

I prepare myself for death every day. For us Buddhists, death is something very natural, a phenomenon that is part of the cycle of existence, samsara. Death is not an ending. It is something very familiar for us; we almost instinctively accept it, and we do not need to fear it. I imagine dying to be something like exchanging worn-out clothes for new ones. This could be something wonderful.

Some people, sweet and attractive, and strong and healthy, happen to die young. They are masters in disguise teaching us about impermanence.

Such practices as bodhicitta automatically bring calmness at the time of death. The mind at the time of death is at a very critical period, and if you are able to leave a strong, positive impact at that time, then it will become a very powerful force in continuing a positive experience in the next life.

We are born and reborn countless number of times, and it is possible that each being has been our parent at one time or another. Therefore, it is likely that all beings in this universe have familial connections.

The fact remains that the birth cycles of all sentient beings are beginningless, and that countless times in previous lives we have each fulfilled the role of a mother. The feeling of a mother for her child is a classic example of love.

Sometimes when I think about death I get some kind of excitement. Instead of fear, I have a feeling of curiosity and this makes it much easier for me to accept death. Of course, my only burden if I die today is, "Oh, what will happen to Tibet? What about Tibetan culture? What about the six million Tibetan people's rights?" This is my main concern. Otherwise, I feel almost no fear of death.

Buddhists say that rebirth is a reality. It is a fact. We believe that there is a subtle consciousness which is the source of everything we call the created world. This subtle consciousness abides in each individual from the beginning of time until buddhahood is attained. That is what we call "being." This "being" can take different forms— animal, human, and ultimately buddha.

At the moment of death, the consciousness is influenced by all the intentions and motives, by all the deeds and experiences of the dying person. The repayment for past deeds determines the direction, the course of the next life. What we have done to others will fall back on us in the coming life. This is how the consciousness continues to exist and is reborn together with the accumulated karma in a new body.

I often reflect on my own situation as the Dalai Lama. I am sure there are people who are prepared to sacrifice their lives for me. But when my death comes, I have to face it alone. They cannot help me at all. Even my own body has to be left behind. I will travel to the next life under the power of my own actions. So what is it that will help us? Only the imprints of positive actions left on our minds.

EQUALITY OF HUMAN BEINGS

In essence, all beings are united by the desire to gain happiness and avoid suffering. We are also the same in that it is possible to remove suffering and attain happiness, to which we all have an equal right. Then what is the difference between you and all others?

To some people this may sound naïve, but I would remind them that, no matter what part of the world we come from, fundamentally we are all the same human beings. . . . We have the same basic needs and concerns. Furthermore, all of us human beings want freedom and the right to determine our own destiny as individuals. That is human nature.

Little children do not bother about religion and nationality, rich or poor; they just want to play together. At a young age the sense of oneness of humanity is much more fresh. As we grow older, we make a lot of distinctions; a lot of artificial creations that are actually secondary become more important, and basic human concern diminishes. That is a problem.

Buddhism holds that consciousness penetrates a being at the very moment of conception, and that consequently the embryo is already a living being. This is why we consider abortion to be the same as taking the life of a living being and as such is not a just action. That is what I meant when I spoke of the necessity for nonviolent birth control. However, there can be exceptional situations. I am thinking, for example, of a case where it is certain that the child will be born with abnormalities or where the mother's life is in danger.

Whether we like it or not, we have all been born on this earth as part of one great family. Rich or poor, educated or uneducated, belonging to one nation, religion, ideology, or another, ultimately each of us is just a human being like everyone else. We all desire happiness and do not want suffering. Furthermore, each of us has the same right to pursue happiness and avoid suffering. When you recognize that all beings are equal in this respect, you automatically feel empathy and closeness for them. Out of this, in turn, comes a genuine sense of universal responsibility; the wish to actively help others overcome their problems.

If one American soldier is killed, it is immediately known, but few bother about how many civilians or combatants are killed on the other side. All of the killed are persons, each valuing his own life.

To those who believe in God or in a creator, I ask them to put more emphasis on the equality of all human beings. Forget about other galaxies and concentrate on this globe, this planet. If one creator created all earthly beings, discrimination has no place. There can be no differences on the basis of color, social background, or, particularly in this country, of caste.

When I meet new people in new places, in my mind there is no barrier, no curtain. In my mind, as human beings we are brothers and sisters, there is no difference in substances. I can express whatever I feel, without hesitation, just as to an old friend. With this feeling we can communicate without any difficulty and can contact heart to heart, not with just a few nice words, but really heart to heart.

RELIGION

This is my simple religion. There is no need for temples; no need for complicated philosophy. Our own brain, our own heart is our temple; the philosophy is kindness.

Religion shows that despite all the sorrowful experiences there is still an indestructible ultimate meaning. In a mysterious way, religion gives humanity the gift of a hope stronger than all obstacles, than all afflictions.

The common factor among all religions is that, whatever the philosophical differences between them, they are primarily concerned with helping their followers become better human beings. Consequently, all religions encourage the practice of kindness, generosity, and concern for others.

Since I've become a refugee, I have had more opportunity to have closer contact with other traditions, mainly through individuals, and I have gained a much deeper understanding of their value. As a result, my attitude now is that each one is a valid religion. I still believe that Buddhist philosophy is more sophisticated, that is has more variety or is more vast, but all other religions still have tremendous benefits or great potential. . . . Today, wherever I go and whenever I meet someone who follows a different religion, I deeply admire their practice and I very sincerely respect their tradition.

All of the different religious faiths, despite their philosophical differences, have a similar objective. Every religion emphasizes human improvement, love, respect for others, sharing other people's suffering. On these lines every religion has more or less the same viewpoint and the same goal.

Without accepting a religion, but simply developing a realization of the importance of compassion and love, and with more concern and respect for others, a kind of spiritual development is very possible for those persons who are outside of religion.

We must try to promote harmony among various religious traditions. It is important for followers of each tradition to practice sincerely and seriously. Suppose we are Buddhists. In order to promote human values, we must, first, make every effort to improve ourselves. In that way, we will prove to be a good example to others. Instead of thinking of conversion, we would think about how much we can contribute through our tradition.

All religions share a common root, which is limitless compassion. They emphasize human improvement, love, respect for others, and compassion for the suffering of others. Insofar as love is essential in every religion, we could say that love is a universal religion.

It is my belief, for the world in general, that compassion is more important than "religion."

Compassion, tolerance, and altruism bring us happiness and calmness. Therefore, these are basically spiritual. Religion comes later. Actually, religion is meant for satisfaction and is the ultimate source of happiness. It simply tries to strengthen the element of mental happiness. Perhaps positive mental thought is my conception of spirituality.

All religious traditions talk about methods of compassion and forgiveness. If we accept religion, we should take the religious methods seriously and sincerely and use them in our daily lives. Then, a meaningful life can develop.

One might say that religion is a kind of luxury. If you have a religion, that is good. But it is clear that even without religion we can manage. However, without basic human qualities such as love, compassion, and kindness, we cannot survive. They are essential to our own peace and mental stability.

The purpose of religion is not to build beautiful churches or temples, but to cultivate positive human qualities such as tolerance, generosity, and love.

The essence of any religion is a good heart. Sometimes I call love and compassion a universal religion. This is my religion. Complicated philosophy, this and that, sometimes creates more trouble and problems. If these sophisticated philosophies are useful for the development of a good heart, then good: use them fully. If these complicated philosophies or systems become an obstacle to a good heart, then it is better to leave them.

I consider it very important for religion to have an influence on politicians. Politicians need religion much more than pious people who have withdrawn from the world need it. There is a constant increase in the scandals in politics and business that can be traced back to the lack of self-discipline on the part of the responsible parties.

It is an absurd assumption that religion and morality have no place in politics and that a man of religion and a believer in morality should seclude himself as a hermit. These ideas lack proper perspective vis-à-vis man's relation to his society and the role of politics in our lives.

What is God? The word God, in one sense, means infinite love. I think Buddhists accept that. But Buddhists do not accept God in the sense of something supreme, in the center, or something absolute, a creator. Buddhists find a lot of contradictions regarding that concept. I think Christians, along with the notion of a creator, accept just one life, this very life, created by God. I think that idea is very powerful, has its own beauty. And that concept, you see, creates a feeling of intimacy with God.

All major religions are basically the same in that they emphasize peace of mind and kindness, but it is very important to practice this in our daily lives, not just in a church or a temple.

The very purpose of religion is to control yourself, not to criticize others. Rather, we must criticize ourselves. How much am I doing about my anger? About my attachment, about my hatred, about my pride, my jealousy? These are the things which we much check in daily life.

Regrettably, religion is frequently used solely as an instrument of power in order to force one's will upon others. In such cases there are certainly not religious motives but very selfish ones at work. Unfortunately, religions have contributed, and continue to contribute, toward increasing separations and hostilities between people. Instead of helping, religion then creates even more problems. Especially today, it appears to me that to spread our own religion is not the most important goal. The dialogue among religions is more important.

A conversion to Buddhism should be thoroughly considered. A spontaneous change of religion has almost always proved to be difficult and can lead to serious emotional disorders. Anyone who converts to Buddhism should be modest and not want to do everything differently from top to bottom with the excessive religious enthusiasm of the convert. This is what we are advised to do by an old Tibetan proverb that tells us: "Change your consciousness, but leave your exterior as it is."

Whoever excludes others will find himself excluded in turn. Those who affirm that their God is the only God are doing something dangerous and pernicious, because they are on the way to imposing their beliefs on others, by any means possible.

In general, I am in favor of people continuing to follow the religion of their own culture and inheritance. Of course, individuals have every right to change if they find that a new religion is more effective or suitable for their spiritual needs. But, generally speaking, it is better to experience the value of one's own religious tradition.

NONVIOLENCE AND PEACE

The awarding of the Nobel Prize to me, a simple monk from far
away Tibet, here in Norway, also fills us Tibetans with hope. It
means that despite the fact that we have not drawn attention to
our plight by means of violence, we have not been forgotten.
It also means that the values we cherish, in particular our respect
for all forms of life and the belief in the power of truth, are today
recognized and encouraged. It is also a tribute to my mentor,
Mahatma Gandhi, whose example is an inspiration to so many
of us.

I am a firm believer in nonviolence, on moral as well as practical
grounds. Using violence against a strong power can be suicidal.
For countries like ours, the only hope for survival is to wage a
nonviolent struggle founded on justice, truth, and unwavering
determination.

We should also remember that once we cultivate a compassionate attitude, nonviolence comes automatically. Nonviolence is not a diplomatic word, it is compassion in action. If you have hatred in your heart, then very often your actions will be violent, whereas if you have compassion in your heart, your actions will be nonviolent.

As long as I lead our freedom struggle, there will be no deviation from the path of nonviolence.

Our compassionate and nonviolent Buddhist culture has much to offer to the rest of the world, and especially to China and the Chinese people, to whom Buddhism is not an alien religion.

In the history of man, it has already been proved that the human will is more powerful than the gun.

The necessary foundation for world peace and the ultimate goal of any new international order is the elimination of violence at every level. For this reason the practice of nonviolence surely suits us all. It simply requires determination, for by its very nature nonviolent action requires patience. While the practice of nonviolence is still something of an experiment on this planet, if it is successful, it will open the way to a far more peaceful world in the next century.

Our planet is blessed with vast natural treasure. If we use them wisely, beginning with the elimination of militarism and war, every human being will be able to live a healthy, prosperous existence. Naturally, global peace cannot occur all at once. All of us, every member of the world community, has a moral responsibility to help avert the immense suffering which results from war and civil strife. We must find a peaceful, nonviolent way for the forces of freedom, truth, and democracy to develop successfully as peoples emerge from oppression.

Everybody loves to talk about calm and peace whether in a family, national, or international context, but without *inner* peace how can we make real peace? World peace through hatred and force is impossible.

The only true guardian of peace lies within: a sense of concern and responsibility for your own future and an altruistic concern for the well-being of others.

Through kindness, whether at our own level or at the national and international level, through mutual understanding and through mutual respect we will get peace, we will get happiness, and we will get genuine satisfaction. It is very difficult to achieve peace and harmony through competition and hatred, so the practice of kindness is very, very important and very, very valuable in human society.

Peace, in the sense of the absence of war, is of little value to someone who is dying of hunger or cold. It will not remove the pain of torture inflicted on a prisoner of conscience. It does not comfort those who have lost their loved ones in floods caused by senseless deforestation in a neighboring country. Peace can only last where human rights are respected, where the people are fed, and where individuals and nations are free.

The difficult task of nuclear disarmament remains. For as long as there are such weapons, a disaster is still possible because we are constantly at the mercy of a handful of irresponsible people. As for me, I still advocate what I call inner disarmament through the reduction of hatred and the promotion of compassion.

At the time of the Persian Gulf crisis I made an inner pledge—a commitment that for the rest of my life I would contribute to furthering the idea of demilitarization. As far as my own country is concerned, I have made up my mind that in the future, Tibet should be a completely demilitarized zone. Once again, in working to bring about demilitarization, the key factor is human compassion.

Our long-term responsibility—everyone's responsibility, whether they are believers or nonbelievers—is to find ways to promote a peaceful and compassionate society. I think one way is quite simple. Each individual must try to ensure peace and compassion in his family. Put together ten peaceful, compassionate homes, or one hundred, and that's a community. . . .We might have one or two setbacks, but generally I think we could develop a sensible society. Sensible here means a sense of community, a sense of responsibility, and a sense of commitment.

Today we are so interdependent that the concept of war has become outdated. When we face problems or disagreements today, we have to arrive at solutions through dialogue. Dialogue is the only appropriate method. One-sided victory is no longer relevant. We must work to resolve conflicts in a spirit of reconciliation and always keep in mind the interests of others. We cannot destroy our neighbors! We cannot ignore their interests! Doing so would ultimately cause us to suffer. I therefore think that the concept of violence is now unsuitable. Nonviolence is the appropriate method.

The Iraq issue is becoming very critical now. War, or the kind of organized fighting, is something that came with the development of human civilization. . . . Unfortunately, although we are in the 21st century, we still have not been able to get rid of the habit of our older generations. I am talking about the belief or confidence that we can solve our problems with arms. It is because of this notion that the world continues to be dogged by all kinds of problems. But what can we do? What can we do when big powers have already made up their minds? All we can do is to pray for a gradual end to the tradition of wars.

WESTERN CIVILIZATION

Western countries are never satisfied. They have everything, and they still want more. Other countries, like Ethiopia, suffer from chronic famine. They have nothing, and tomorrow they will have less than nothing. We must act to close this ever-increasing gap, and bring together the developed and less developed worlds so they meet on comparable ground, if not on a basis of equality. Yes, this should be our priority.

Western education is almost solely oriented toward the development of intelligence and the accumulation of as much knowledge as possible. In this process the development of the heart is probably neglected. . . . There must be a balance between the brain and the heart. I think that a heartless human being with a very well-functioning brain is a dangerous troublemaker. I value someone more whose intelligence is less developed but who has a good heart.

Western civilizations these days place great importance on filling the human "brain" with knowledge, but no one seems to care about filling the human "heart" with compassion. This is what the real role of religion is.

Western civilization is very advanced on the material level. If it were as fertile in developing techniques for inner development as it is in developing technology, it would be at the forefront of the modern world. But when man forgets to cultivate his inner life, he turns himself into a machine and becomes a slave to material things. Then he is a human being only in name.

In the Western world, with its affluence, a great fear, a strong feeling of emptiness and pointlessness, often hides beneath the beautiful surface of the "good life," because people take the material world too seriously. Those who succumb to the illusion that they can buy the meaning of life grow unhappy. Technology, science, and progress only make the outer conditions of life easier; they do not change any of the fundamental human problems. There is still suffering, poverty, and fear.

Perhaps in monasteries in the West there is leisure, but outside—
especially in the cities—life seems to be running at a rapid pace,
like a clock, never stopping for an instant! So if you look at life
in an urban community, it seems as if every aspect of a person's
life has to be so precise, designed like a screw that has to fit exactly
in the hole. In some sense, you have no control over your own life.
In order to survive, you have to follow this pattern and the pace
that is set for you.

I am convinced that Western science with its logical thinking has
made an important contribution to solving the age-old problems
of humanity. Will these new findings and discoveries, however,
be used for the benefit of humanity or for its destruction? Today,
the nightmare of the entire globe being destroyed with one strike
could become a reality. But in recent decades, Western thinking has
changed considerably. Many scientists have told me in conversation
that they are proceeding from a new point of view that embraces the
world as a whole. In their view, thinking and feeling should no longer
be poles apart.

MATERIALISM AND
THE MODERN WORLD

When our attitude towards our material possessions and wealth is not proper, it can lead to an extreme attachment towards such things as our property, houses and belongings. This can lead to an inability to feel contented. If that happens, then one will always remain in a state of dissatisfaction, always wanting more. In a way, one is then really poor, because the suffering of poverty is the suffering of wanting something and feeling the lack of it.

If an individual has a sufficient spiritual base, he won't let himself be overwhelmed by the lure of technology and by the madness of possession. He or she will know how to find the right balance, without asking for too much, and know how to say: I have a camera, that's enough, I don't want another. The constant danger is to open the door to greed, one of our most relentless enemies. It is here that the real work of the mind is put into practice.

All too frequently, wealth does not give us a happy and contented life. On the contrary, many rich people become slaves to their money because they are constantly worried about trying to increase their possessions. As a result they live in a continually hectic state. They do not know serenity and equanimity toward material things. When we live in such a world of restlessness, it is important to distance ourselves time and again and rediscover our inner peace.

In the frenzy of modern life we lose sight of the real value of humanity. People become the sum total of what they produce. Human beings act like machines whose function is to make money. . . . Humans are not for money, money is for humans. We need enough to live, so money is necessary, but we also need to realize that if there is too much attachment to wealth, it does not help at all. As the saints of India and Tibet tell us, the wealthier one becomes, the more suffering one endures.

Lack of contentment—which really comes down to greed—sows the seed of envy and aggressive competitiveness, and leads to a culture of excessive materialism. The negative atmosphere this creates becomes the context for all kinds of social ills which bring suffering to all members of that community.

Recently I met another group of scientists in America who said that the rate of mental illness in their country was quite high, around 12 percent of the population. It became clear during our discussion that depression was caused not by a lack of material necessities but more likely by a difficulty in giving and receiving affection.

Material things usually correspond to physical happiness, whereas spiritual development corresponds to mental happiness. Since our "I" has these two aspects—physical and mental—we need an inseparable combination of material progress and internal, or spiritual, progress. Balancing these is crucial to utilizing material progress and inner development for the good of human society.

We have, in my view, created a society in which people find it harder and harder to show one another basic affection. In place of the sense of community and belonging, which we find such a reassuring feature of less wealthy (and generally rural) societies, we find a high degree of loneliness and alienation. . . . Modern industrial society often strikes me as being like a huge self-propelled machine. Instead of human beings in charge, each individual is a tiny, insignificant component with no choice but to move when the machine moves.

A clear distinction should be made between what is not found by science and what is found to be nonexistent by science. What science finds to be nonexistent, we must accept as nonexistent; but what science merely does not find is a completely different matter. . . . It is quite clear that there are many, many mysterious things.

Today I see encouraging signs that science does not have to stand in contradiction to religion and spirituality. In the past few years, I have discovered this in conversations with biologists, psychologists, quantum physicists, and cosmologists. We frequently spoke about how there is a relationship between the findings of natural science, the human mind, and the human soul.

Who could fail to be impressed at our ability to land people on the moon? Yet the fact remains that if, for example, we were to go to a nuclear physicist and say, "I am facing a moral dilemma, what should I do?" he or she could only shake their head and suggest we look elsewhere for an answer.

With the ever-growing impact of science on our lives, religion and spirituality have a greater role to play in reminding us of our humanity. There is no contradiction between the two. Each gives us valuable insights into the other. Both science and the teachings of the Buddha tell us of the fundamental unity of all things.

On a wider scale, we might also consider the growing appreciation of fundamental human rights all over the world. This represents a very positive development in my view. The way in which the international community generally responds to natural disasters with immediate aid is also a wonderful feature of the modern world.

When the media focuses too closely on the negative aspects of human nature, there is a danger that we become persuaded that violence and aggression are its principal characteristics. This is a mistake, I believe. The fact that violence is newsworthy suggests the very opposite. Good news is not remarked on precisely because there is so much of it. Consider that at any given moment there must be hundreds of millions of acts of kindness taking place around the world. Although there will undoubtedly be many acts of violence in progress at the same time, their number is surely very much less. If therefore, the media is to be ethically responsible, it needs to reflect this simple fact.

In this modern age, when it comes to dealing with economic situations, there are no longer familial or even national boundaries. From country to country and continent to continent, the world is inextricably interconnected. Each country depends heavily on the others. In order for a country to develop its own economy, it is forced to take seriously into account the economic conditions of other countries as well. In fact, economic improvement in other countries ultimately results in economic improvement in one's own country.

Modern society does not accord humility the place it had in Tibet when I was young. Then, both our culture and peoples' basic admiration of humility provided a climate in which it flourished. . . . Yet in contemporary life, humility is more important than ever. The more successful we humans become, both as individuals and as a family through our development of science and technology, the more essential it becomes to preserve humility. For the greater our temporal achievements, the more vulnerable we become to pride and arrogance.

The challenge we face is therefore to find some means of enjoying the same degree of harmony and tranquility as those more traditional communities while benefiting fully from the material developments of the world as we find it at the dawn of a new millennium.

THE ENVIRONMENT

I often joke that the moon and stars look beautiful, but if any of us tried to live on them we would be miserable. This blue planet of ours is a delightful habitat. Its life is our life, its future our future. Indeed, the earth acts like a mother to us all. Like children, we are dependent on her. In the face of such global problems as the greenhouse effect and depletion of the ozone layer, individual organizations and single nations are helpless. Unless we all work together, no solution can be found. Our mother earth is teaching us a lesson in universal responsibility.

This planet is our home. Taking care of our world and of our planet is like looking after our own home. In a way, one can say that the earth is our mother. She is so good that whatever we do, she puts up with it. But now the time has come when our destructive power is so vast that our mother is obliged to call us to account. Isn't the population explosion alone not a clear sign of this? Nature itself has limits.

Only if we live in a modest and sensible manner and do not waste the earth's natural resources are we living in harmony with nature. If we do not stop the destructive exploitation, the natural equilibrium will be disturbed, the number of natural catastrophes will increase, and not only humanity but also the animal and plant world will suffer as a result.

When the environment changes, the climatic condition also changes. When the climate changes dramatically, the economy and many other things change. Our physical health will be greatly affected. Again, conservation is not merely a question of morality, but a question of our own survival.

No one knows what will happen in a few decades or a few centuries, what adverse effect, for example, deforestation might have on the weather, the soil, the rain.

In order to achieve more effective results and in order to succeed in the protection, conservation, and preservation of the natural environment, first of all, I think, it is also important to bring about internal balance within human beings themselves.

Tapping the limited resources of our world—particularly those of the developing nations—simply to fuel consumerism is disastrous. If it continues unchecked, eventually we will all suffer. We must respect the delicate matrix of life and allow it to replenish itself.

As people alive today, we must consider future generations: a clean environment is a human right like any other. It is therefore part of our responsibility toward others to ensure that the world we pass on is as healthy, if not healthier, than we found it.

TIBET

Tibet is distinguished by its extraordinary geography, the unique race and language of its people, and the rich culture they have developed over 2,100 years of recorded history. Approximately six million Tibetans populate our country, which covers around 2.5 million square kilometers, an area the size of Western Europe.

In the Tibetan culture, our relations with nature, including animals, were very peaceful. We lived in great harmony with nature. At its foundation and thereafter, after the arrival of Buddhism in Tibet, Tibetan society in general was characterized by compassion and openness. It was a society where people felt at ease. For those reasons I believe it might serve as an example.

We Tibetans complain over the fact that China invaded our country and now colonize it. But this isn't because we hate the Chinese. They provided us with a supreme test of courage. Now it is time for them to leave.

Fundamentally, the issue of Tibet is political. It is an issue of colonial rule: the oppression of Tibet by the People's Republic of China and resistance to that rule by the people of Tibet. This issue can be resolved only through negotiations and not, as China would have it, through force, intimidation, and population transfer.

In spite of the fact that we Tibetans have to oppose Communist China, I can never bring myself to hate her people. Hatred is not a sign of strength but of weakness. . . . How can we hate millions of Chinese, who have no power and are helplessly led by their leaders? We cannot even hate the Chinese leaders, for they have suffered tremendously for their nation and the cause which they believe to be right. I do not believe in hatred, but I do believe, as I have always done, that one day truth and justice will prevail.

Violations of human rights in Tibet have a distinct character. Such abuses are aimed at Tibetans as a people from asserting their own identity and their wish to preserve it. Thus, human rights violations in Tibet are often the result of institutionalized racial and cultural discrimination.

Diversity and traditions can never justify the violations of human rights. Thus, discrimination of persons from a different race, of women, and of weaker sections of society may be traditional in some regions, but if they are inconsistent with universally recognized human rights, these forms of behavior must change.

Brute force, no matter how strongly applied, can never subdue the basic human desire for freedom and dignity.

In spite of the very serious, harsh, repressive nature of what is happening in Tibet today, basically, I am very hopeful, because the overall situation in the world is that the totalitarian communist way of ruling does not work. And then in China the democratic movement not only survived, but is now very active.

For fourteen years we have been trying very seriously to negotiate with China on the Tibetan question, but even after making many concessions our efforts have been in vain. It has become clear, therefore, that pressure on China from the international community is indispensable. Our own experience has shown that our efforts have yielded no concrete results; hence the importance of such worldwide pressure.

The Tibetan people have a deep trust, believing that the Dalai Lama will bring freedom to them. But I am only a Buddhist monk. I have only the strength of compassion, and the strength that my cause is a just cause.

Even if the Chinese leave nothing but ashes in our sacred land, Tibet will rise from these ashes as a free country even if it takes a long time to do so. No imperialist power has succeeded in keeping other people in colonial subjection for long.

The Tibetan struggle is also a nonviolent struggle. We take our inspiration from the teachings of love and compassion of the Buddha, and from the practice of nonviolence of the great leaders, Mahatma Gandhi and Martin Luther King. For me, the path of nonviolence is a matter of principle, and my stand on this is absolutely firm.

Not a single hour in the day goes by without my thinking about the situation in Tibet, and of my people imprisoned in their mountain fortress. . . . Although I am a refugee I remain free, free to speak on behalf of my people. I am more useful in the free world as a spokesman for Tibet. I can serve my country better from exile.

SPIRITUAL GUIDANCE

In a sense a religious practitioner, whether man or woman, is like a soldier engaged in combat. Who is the enemy? Ignorance, anger, attachment, and pride are the ultimate enemies; they are not outside, but within, and must be fought with the weapons of wisdom and meditative concentration.

I profoundly believe that real spiritual change comes about not by merely praying or wishing that all negative aspects of our minds disappear and all positive aspects blossom. It is only by our concerted effort, an effort based on an understanding of how the mind and its various emotional and psychological states interact, that we bring about true spiritual progress.

I normally recommend to Buddhist practitioners not to see every action of their spiritual teacher as divine and noble. There are specific, very demanding qualities that are required of a spiritual mentor. You don't simply say, "It is good behavior because it is the guru's." This is never done. You should recognize the unwholesome as being unwholesome, so one might infer that it is worthwhile to criticize it.

The guru, the spiritual teacher, is responsible for his or her improper behavior. It is the student's responsibility not to be drawn into it. The blame is on both. Partly it is because the student is too obedient and devoted to the spiritual master—a kind of blind acceptance of that person's guidance. . . . But of course part of the blame lies with the spiritual master, because he lacks the integrity that is necessary to be immune to that kind of vulnerability.

If students sincerely point out the faults of the guru and explain any contradictory behavior, this will, in fact, help the guru to correct that behavior and adjust any wrong actions.

It is said that one should be willing to scrutinize a teacher for as long as twelve years to ensure that he or she is qualified. I don't think that this is time wasted. On the contrary, the more clearly we come to see the qualities of a teacher, the more valuable he or she is to us. If we are hasty and devote ourselves to someone unqualified, the results are often disastrous. So, take time to scrutinize your potential teachers, be they Buddhist or of some other faith.

Fame, wealth, and power are not qualifications for a spiritual teacher! It is spiritual knowledge we must be sure the teacher possesses, knowledge of the doctrine he or she is to teach as well as experiential knowledge derived from practice and life led.

We must take direct responsibility for our own spiritual lives and rely upon nobody and nothing, for even the Buddhas of the ten directions and three times are unable to help us if we do not help ourselves. If another being were able to save us, surely he would already have done so. It is time, therefore, that we help ourselves.

THE ROLE OF
THE DALAI LAMA

My most important school was life itself, with its enormous challenges and the many difficulties that my people have to face. My fate as a refugee has frequently brought me into desperate, almost hopeless situations. It has constantly forced me to confront naked reality. Under this constant pressure, I time and again have had to prove my outer decisiveness and my inner strength. This was above all about not losing courage and hope. The daily meditation and my life experience are the two areas to which I probably owe the greatest debt.

As the Dalai Lama, my main concern is Tibet and six million of the country's people. As a Buddhist monk, I have to try to be concerned with means to contribute to the welfare of all beings—even insects and animals—and particularly, humanity. Third, as a human being, I always feel that today we need the realization of oneness of all human beings.

When people come to listen to me, many do so with the intention to get a message or a technique for securing inner peace and for achieving a successful life. Some people may have come simply out of curiosity, but the important thing is that we should know we are all the same, all human beings. I am nothing special: I am just a simple Buddhist monk. Just one human being. And we all have the potential for good as well as for bad.

My path is that of a monk. This means that I follow the 235 vows for a monk. The four main vows prohibit a monk from killing, stealing, and lying about his spiritual knowledge. A monk must also strictly keep the vow of chastity. These rules free me from many distractions and worries of everyday life.

The Dalai Lama is an individual, and even the institution of the Dalai Lama came into being at a certain stage of Tibet's history. In the future it may disappear, but the Tibetan nation will always remain.

A new Dalai Lama will appear when the circumstances call for him. But if history takes a different course, we must also accept this. Political systems change; the only thing that never changes is the human heart, the longing for happiness, the striving for freedom. These are the true reasons for continued development and progress, whether in the material realm or the spiritual. This is also true for my Tibetan people.

I am a seventy-year-old Buddhist monk and in a few months I will be seventy-one. The greater part of my life has not been happy. . . . When I was fifteen I lost my freedom; at the age of twenty-four I lost my country. Now, forty-one years have passed since I became a refugee and news from my homeland is always very saddening. Yet inside, my mental state seems quite peaceful. Bad news tends to go in one ear and out the other; not much remains stuck within my mind. The result is that my peace of mind is not too disturbed.

The task of man is to help others; that's my firm teaching, that's my message. That is my own belief. For me, the fundamental question is better relations; better relations among human beings—and whatever I can contribute to that.

[This is] a short prayer which gives me great inspiration and determination:

> *For as long as space endures,*
>
> *And for as long as living beings remain,*
>
> *Until then may I, too, abide*
>
> *To dispel the misery of the world.*

Looking back over my life, I can say with full confidence that such things as the office of Dalai Lama, the political power it confers, even the comparative wealth it puts at my disposal, contribute not even a fraction to my feelings of happiness compared with the happiness I have felt on those occasions when I have been able to benefit others.

CHRONOLOGY

DECEMBER 17, 1933—The 13th Dalai Lama, Thupten Gyatso, dies in Lhasa at the age of 57.

JULY 6, 1935—Lhamo Thondup, the future 14th Dalai Lama, is born in Taktser, Amdo, Tibet. He is the ninth child born to his mother but only the fifth child to survive. His mother gave birth to sixteen children in all, seven of whom survived.

1937—Lhamo Thondup is recognized as the reincarnation of the 13th Dalai Lama.

FEBRUARY 22, 1940—Lhamo Thondup is enthroned as the 14th Dalai Lama in Lhasa. He is soon inducted as a novice monk and changes his name to Jamphel Ngawang Lobsang Yeshe Tenzin Gyatso. He begins his monastic education at the age of five. His formal education lasts for close to twenty years.

OCTOBER 1950—China invades Tibet.

NOVEMBER 17, 1950—The Dalai Lama, at the age of fifteen, assumes full temporal leadership of Tibet.

MAY 1951—Seventeen-Point Agreement is signed between China and Tibet under duress. The Agreement makes Tibet a "national autonomous region" of China.

JULY 1954 TO JUNE 1955—The Dalai Lama visits China to meet with Mao Zedong and other Chinese leaders for peace talks.

NOVEMBER 1956 TO MARCH 1957—The Dalai Lama visits India for the commemoration of 2,500 years of Buddhism. He meets with Nehru and other Indian leaders.

MARCH 10, 1959—Thousands of Tibetans take to the streets and surround Norbulingka Palace in an anti-Chinese revolt. The uprising is in response to an apparent plan of the Chinese to capture the Dalai Lama at a theatrical performance.

MARCH 17, 1959—The Dalai Lama escapes at night from Norbulingka Palace in Lhasa and flees to India where he seeks asylum; 80,000 Tibetans follow him into exile.

MARCH 1959—The uprising in Lhasa is suppressed. Thousands of Tibetans are executed and imprisoned. Martial law is declared.

1965—The Cultural Revolution begins. Approximately 90% of the remaining monasteries are destroyed and Tibetan customs, culture, and religion are outlawed. More than a quarter of a million monks and nuns are forced to give up their religious life, and more than 100,000 are the victims of abuse, torture, and murder.

1976—The Cultural Revolution ends with the death of Mao. The Chinese admit "past mistakes in Tibet." Martial law is lifted and a program to promote more religious freedoms is begun in Tibet by the Chinese. The Dalai Lama comments that the religious freedoms that are promised "are simply empty talk."

1979—The Dalai Lama has first contact with Chinese government since his exile in 1959. China allows the Dalai Lama's delegates to visit Tibet.

1983—The Dalai Lama sends delegates to negotiate in Beijing. The talks collapse the following year.

1987—The Dalai Lama proposes Five Point Peace Plan to members of Congress during visit to Washington D.C.

1988—The Dalai Lama delivers Strasbourg Proposal to members of European Parliament. Proposal offers the Chinese control of foreign policy and defense in exchange for complete internal autonomy. The Chinese agree to negotiate with him.

MARCH 1989—In response to pro-independence demonstrations, martial law is imposed in Tibet. Hundreds of people are killed and thousands are arrested.

DECEMBER 10, 1989—The Dalai Lama is awarded the Nobel Peace Prize in Oslo, Norway.

MAY 1990—Martial law is lifted in Tibet, but security forces still are free to arrest, detain, or torture anyone they suspect of subversive activities.

1991—China declares that Tibet is "open" to foreign investment.

1995—China denounces the six-year-old boy who has been recognized by the Dalai Lama as the 11th Panchen Lama (the most important spiritual leader in Tibet after the Dalai Lama) and selects its own candidate. The boy, Gandun Chokyi Nyima, and his entire family are believed to be under house arrest.

1996—China bans displaying photos of the Dalai Lama.

2004—The Dalai Lama's envoys return from Beijing after their third visit in recent years attempting to reopen dialogue with the Chinese government.

OCTOBER 17, 2007—The US Congress and President George W. Bush award the Dalai Lama the Congressional Gold Medal, the nation's highest civilian honor.

2011—The Dalai Lama officially transfers his formal political power to a democratically elected prime minister.

2012—The John Templeton Foundation awards the Dalai Lama the Templeton Prize, honoring his dedication to science, ethics, nonviolence, and his universal message of compassion.

JULY 6, 2018—The Dalai Lama celebrates his 83rd birthday.